Catwalk

ISBN: 978-0-578-64422-6

Longship Press

Longship Press is an independent small-press publishing company.
1122 4th Street, San Rafael, California 94901

Catwalk

Meryl Natchez

LONGSHIP PRESS :: SAN RAFAEL :: CALIFORNIA

Acknowledgments

Some of these poems appeared in the following journals and anthologies: *American Journal of Poetry, Atlanta Review, California Quarterly, Canary, Clean Sheets, Literary Matters, The Moth, Nostos Literary Journal, Oberon, Poetry Northwest, The Rappahanock Review, Sixfold, Tar River Poetry Review, West Trestle Review, Winning Writers, Writing in a Woman's Voice, Coffee Poems Anthology,* World Enough Writers, 2019; *Cooking with the Muse,* Tupelo Press, 2017; *America, We Call Your Name,* Sixteen Rivers Press, 2018. Thanks to the generous editors.

Notes on the Poems

The couplet sonnets in this collection are inspired by Jericho Brown's essay on a form he calls the Duplex. His rules are rigorous, with specifics on echoing lines and rhyme. My rules are derived from his but much looser; as an homage to Jericho Brown, I call my form the Looseplex.

Many of the prose poems in this collection were inspired by Carlo Rovelli's lush, literate explanations of the history and current state of physics, *Seven Brief Lessons on Physics* and *Why Reality is Not What It Seems.*

Cover Art and Design

The cover art is a painting by Maureen Solomon, *Catwalk,* oil on canvas, with our many thanks. Book design by Lawrence Tjernell.

Contents

Heart of the Matter

Looseplex: Rescue Mission

The goldfinches arrived; I flew to New York.
A secondhand store of dubious

> Edges, unforeseen drops, another black, bleak
> reconstructed while we sleep, something awry.

Hope, that glitters like pyrite under water.
Metallic smell of rain on asphalt.

> Her furniture turned to a heap of splinters.
> No degrees: there is hope and there is no hope.

Grief flings its implacable lasso
Off the edge of the world where you will be lost.

> Dante's Hell, where is it? How much does it weigh?
> Fireworks bloom damply from the river

Reluctant to give up on the bent, the broken
Fear that she is totally lost and may not

The Handbook

I wonder how many of us, long hair parted in the middle
poured over the *Chinese Barefoot Doctor's Manual*
by the light of a kerosene lantern,
hoping it was accurate
as we assembled the package
of blankets, twine, cloth diapers and pins,
sleeper, boiled scissors,
wrapped it in newspaper,
tied it, baked it,
and set it on a high shelf,
as we waited for the
unpredictable journey.
Everything we did
needed a handbook then.
So when the head appeared
after more pain than I had
been led to expect,
and Larry rotated
first one shoulder
then the other
and the scrawny body
popped into his arms
just as the handbook said
with an alien beauty
the book hadn't described
is it a surprise that we thought
we were changing the world?
or a surprise
how it pushed back
and changed us?

Two-step, Starting with a Grapefruit

His rape and pillage
to my delicate evisceration.
His silence
to my effusion.
His eye roll
to my "let's talk."
My HBO
to his ESPN.
My Tarot
to his spreadsheet.
My flash of lace
to his flap of cotton.
His torque
to my rack and pinion.
Hip pad
to hip bone
skin against skin
sweat
mingled
and laundered,
tumbled dry.

Full Circle, A Diptych *(with thanks to Forrest Gander)*

For which it turns out you are the cause:
here they are, flawed human beings with adult problems,

their own ways of slicing it, their own patterns and opinions,
with their own lives, their own ways of salting meat.

And helped out with grad school and they're launched.
And endured the teenage years, and paid for college.

To swim, to read, you've paid for the orthodontist,
and they learn to walk.

Massages, spicy food, uninterrupted thought—
you give up nightlife, adult conversation, another hour-and-a-half

and you would do anything for them, and you do:
in a convertible on a winding road by an azure sea

more delightful than sex. Not the best meal, not driving fast,
but limpid as soap bubbles, and there has never been anything

but their fontanel in your neck and you cover it with kisses.
Towards you they smile, they nuzzle the soft bones,

they begin to know who you are. They reach their chubby arms.
They bend when you try to cut their shrimp-shell nails

so fragile, and you swoon before their transparent skin.
The soft floss of their hair, the bluish pattern that blooms.

And wander the few rooms your life has narrowed to,
and when she cries, you pick her up again.

You can hardly bear the baby's ruthless gums,
sleep-deprived, disoriented, your nipples so sore.

Full Circle, A Diptych

Sleep-deprived, disoriented, your nipples so sore
you can hardly bear the baby's ruthless gums,

and when they cry, you pick them up again,
and wander the few rooms your life has narrowed to,

the soft floss of their hair, the bluish pattern that blooms
under transparent skin, shrimp-shell fingernails so fragile

they bend when you try to cut them. Soon
they begin to know who you are, they reach their chubby arms

towards you, they smile, they nuzzle the soft bones
of their fontanel into your neck and cover it with kisses

limpid as soap bubbles, and there has never been anything
more delightful, not sex, not the best meal, not driving fast

in a convertible on a winding road by an azure sea,
and you would do anything for them, and you do,

give up nightlife, adult conversation, hour-and-a-half
massages, spicy food, uninterrupted thought,

and they learn to walk,
to swim, to read, and you've paid for the orthodontist

and endured the teenage years, and paid for college
and helped out with grad school and they're launched,

with their own lives, their own ways of salting meat,
their own ways of slicing it, their own partners and opinions,

here they are, flawed human beings with adult problems
for which it turns out you are the cause.

Gemstone

Years of drips in just one spot
scar the worn enamel of the sink
one drip at a time
until the powdered glass unfuses its mineral
bond, laying bare the iron underneath,
one black star of use.
So, after forty years your essence
reveals itself: familiar, flawed,
hardened by wear—the one I fell for
before I knew anything, glove
to my hand, derringer in my pocket,
sand in my oyster, four decades
polished to pearl.

A Good Lie

A good lie, Francesca says casually, about telling the children the
grasshoppers die instantly as the tarantula sucks out their guts. But
it wakes the image of my mother and her mother and their ongoing
intricate, convoluted prevarications. How I would listen to my
mother on the phone as her stories morphed with each telling, the
startlement when I heard her elaborate a real incident into radiant
fantasy, so that for years I forswore all lies, no "good morning," or
"pleased to meet you." How could I know? Still, I can't escape my
heritage, passed down like china or silver, and when my cat's paw
swells the Saturday before we leave for two weeks, and I call one
vet and then another until I get to one I haven't seen in years, and
they ask: Which cat, Yoda or Gecko, I just say, Yoda. And when
the vet says how eager he is to meet a 24-year-old cat, instead of
coming clean, I invent a story about how this cat is Yoda's kitten,
get tangled when I mention he was a rescue, and elaborate from
there—my mouth far beyond my brain, my grown daughter
watching and I, myself, watching this in astonishment, the lies so
absurd and convoluted and unnecessary they baffle even me.

You think you've shed
the tangle of your past till
you're caught in its undertow.

Apology to Mrs. Joliff 47 years too late

If there is ever an accounting
Mrs. Joliff will not accuse me,
though I'm fairly sure
I was the one that jostled her
on the way to the buffet
that first evening out
after she'd recovered
from a broken hip.

I still see her on the floor
of the swanky spot where they'd brought us
to celebrate. Mr. Joliff crouched beside her
in his suit and tie, holding her hand.
I hear her quiet moans as she said
she knew she'd broken the other hip.
She knew what it felt like.

At 19, what did I know
of porous bones, of injury?
My skin radiated health.
Maybe this was why they chose us
as dining partners, my brother and I, children
of an old friend; we barely knew them.
They were utterly square.

So we didn't stay to wait
for the ambulance, easily accepting
Mr. Joliff's protestations
that there was nothing
we could do.

There was nothing we could do.
We were 19 and 25.

And I can forgive myself
for that, and even for my rush
to grab more food
from the sumptuous spread
that might have caused her fall.

But afterwards, I never even tried
to visit her. Didn't send a card
or a flower, didn't think of her again
for years, so enraptured
with the drama
of my life unfolding.

The Fight

I didn't know my brother could die
in the middle of our fight,

the diagnosis one more barb
perfectly fashioned to wound.

As I sat by his hospital bed, we tried to reclaim
those companionable Cambridge years

when we learned to wash our own laundry,
books strewn on the beds.

How he taught me to wait for the boy
to unlock the car door, then swing both legs in together,

how to play pinball,
how much spice to add to the sauce.

The fight simmered, a stock pot
pushed to the back of the stove

while we waited for him to get better.
Even when his legs began to hold fluids,

and the nurses shook their heads,
I was waiting for the last-minute reversal.

I didn't understand. Death
cuts off the discussion

whether you're finished or not.

Anniversary of My Mother's Death

Because you were so good at making sense of dreams
I thought you would come back in one
at least to let me know
that the way
I helped you die
was exactly what you had asked for.
Or that you never lose your purse now,
that you no longer need notes
to remind you of your notes.

I walk by the West End Suprette,
and look up at your building,
no longer yours.

It seems
I am alone,
no one's daughter.

Last night I dreamt that Micah and I
were putting together a plastic model
of a torso. We found the ribs and heart,
but spread before us were so many parts
that didn't fit.

If you were here, I know
you would make sense of this,
together we would reassemble
the Anatomical Man
and I would not wake
3000 miles from where I grew up,
without you.

Children

you can't imagine
life without them
so asphyxiatingly present
no moment free of their need

till suddenly
you are free
from the longing
to be free

on a shore
untroubled to the horizon
deep in folds of blue

Carnac the Magnificent

Back when marriage was for keeps
my mother-in-law watched Johnny every night.
He came on at eleven, flickering his monologue
onto the desolate late-night air waves as Mabel sat
quilting in her empty living room.
Not much happened in her day
or was likely in the next, her grown son
set against fulfilling his promise,
her husband wheelchaired for life.
But Johnny made her laugh, his
shy, Midwestern corn, his string
of ruinous marriages,
the zany turban and outrageous animals.
One time she knit and sent
a red acrylic crotch cozy, plumped
with tissue paper, an exercise
requiring some imagination as to the size
and shape of his unmentionables
I wonder how many of those he got
from women knitting by the light of the TV
in Omaha or Wichita or Bend?
She never heard back.

Skull of a Small Mammal

The bleached skull sits on the kitchen counter,
provenance unknown.
The teeth could make a necklace
for a Pomo bride—their points delicate
and deadly, a reminder that
the untamed continues to exist
despite the microwave,
the disposal. The savage lurks
above the sink, the dying
fly, the primitive flash I feel
when you leave the good knife unwashed.
I could almost use it on you,
you, the one I love most
when I am able to think,
when my fangs retract a moment,
when my fur remembers your fingers.

Motherhood

I like it that they give robot babies to teens
to simulate parenthood,
that the robots are programmed
to cry unless they are held. I think
the teen mother has to hold them—no one
else can make them shut off—but maybe
I'm imagining that, maybe that's a level of need
only real babies demonstrate. Because
a robot can't prepare you.
Even if it cries all the time,
it isn't wired
into your nervous system. You can't imagine
the despair and rage snarled
within the besotted adoration
that tiny body wrenches from you
at birth.

This is the blood vow,
the one you cannot break.
You can barely acknowledge
even to yourself, the force
of the urge for escape,
so that you're lying if you say
you don't understand
how anyone
can bash a baby's brains
against a wall.
With luck,
you don't do it.

The Museum of Broken Relationships

My favorite exhibit is the axe with the blue head,
the one he used to smash the chairs and tables
she'd left, her things without her.
He shattered one each day until her furniture
became a heap of splinters, bagged and ready for exit.

As when Jacki found out that Will had been cheating
on her all along, that silver-tongued, lying SOB.
She cut the crotch out of all his pants,
tossed them on the lawn and locked the door.
A pair of those would look good here.

And I can remember being crazed with desire,
how his hooded eyes and focused, seductive gaze
made me chase the wrong man,
risk my true love, our children, everything.
As it turned out, he didn't want me.

So my exhibit is one perfect arc of Cabernet
as it left the glass in my hand and streamed
in a slow-motion ribbon through the air between us
to soak his beard and party shirt,
while I strolled off and left him to explain.

Why size has almost nothing to do with it

After the party when you've collapsed on the couch, leaving the
mess for the morning and he gets up as if it were the most natural
thing and fills one sink with soapy water and starts moving the
sponge along each plate and cup until the dishwasher is full,
nothing sexier than his hands dripping soap suds, his love handles
peeping out from his shirt as he moves his fingers up and down,
around and over, nudging the crud from the tines of the forks,
emptying the sink, nothing hotter than the tendons of his arms
as he swabs the counter and when he's done your fatigue has
disappeared and you can't get to him fast enough and even the
longest schlong in Cincinnati can't compete with that.

The Material vs. the Spiritual

On the day when four men carry the taped boxes,
the chairs and tables, the knickknacks down
the steep driveway, pack two trucks and pilot them
through narrow streets to hoist and carry
each object into another house
and stack them in the empty corresponding rooms,
on the day I scurry from one house
to the other, driving my mother's coffee table
to the storage locker with Larry's mother's china,
directing the movers as their shouts
echo up stairwells, down hallways,
while my knees ache and my feet swell,
on the day when there's no hot water and I
can't find the cups, a day when we decide
what to do with each half-full bottle,
the bent trowel, the button
that vaguely reminds me of something that's been
missing it, several hundred scraps of paper
marked by my hand, a stray mothball or two,
it's hard to believe in a life that exists
apart from this one, a transcendent glimmer
as elusive as the slit in the skinny shaft
of the needle, the needle itself buried
in a box whose label I can't decipher,
can't even think about
until I've found, somewhere,
the coffee.

The Population of Loss

Listening to Robert Pinsky's translation
of Dante's *Inferno* as I drive
between the old house and the new,
it occurs to me that moving
is a circle of hell, the one in which you
must examine every object you
have carried with you on the journey of your life,
consider it, judge it, decide its fate.

What to do with my mother's vibrator, for
example, that I found among her things
and saved and tried but didn't like
too much? Toss it out? There's nowhere
to consign a used vibrator, no matter
how top-of-the-line. It finds its way into a box
of odd, unsortable objects
far back in the new closet,
a dark wood if ever there was one,
from which Dante could be eloquent
on my behalf.

Stuck in the Middle with You

Larry is watching the scene with the duct tape
and razor from "Reservoir Dogs,"
grinning and eating pistachios.
I have to look away.

It's the wrong moment for "Lucky,"
the wrong moment for any poem
I might read him, though the calculated,
casual laceration on the screen

is a sort of aria of American violence,
part of our national fabric, like football
and invasion and prizefights

and men have an appetite for it
just as women love the pinch
and pitch of stilettos,
the beauty and pain
part of one package.

Because I have my own
dark pleasures
I turn and wait for another moment,
when my husband's eyes aren't alight
with animal delight

and he is open to a more subtle beauty,
as he so often is,
as both of us so often are,
as we falter together
along the catwalk of consciousness.

Who is this man?

Who is this man who texts me
"I got fish at the market"?

I hardly recognize the dark, troubled poet
I hitched my future to before I knew anything,

the one who recited Pound on a starry hillside
in Canada where we waited out the war.

I understand now why my father was horrified.
What could he see but a boy

set against the powers of the world
who searched for what he couldn't define

knowing only what he couldn't stomach.
I followed him through the years of no money

the seventeen moves, years living outside the law
as babies came and grew,

a little tribe with tangled hair and used clothes.
No one would have predicted

fifty years of rubbing off each other's rough edges
till we seem a placid older couple, our history

invisible except to each other. Who is this gentle,
considerate man, who once left home for days without

calling, who bought books with the rent check,
drove his truck into a tree and walked back with cracked ribs,

who plans our dinner of pink trout and broccolini,
and let's me know that I don't need to shop?

The Ways I See You

flash of the hook
when I rise to the bait

    how eyebrows give the joke away

in your baseball cap
and championship t-shirt

    you with the facts, doing the math

the hard set
your mouth can take

    on the treadmill at the gym, talking to yourself

over breakfast
reading to me from the *Times*

    your willingness to try even swing-dance, even yoga

full black beard
pounding abalone

    gray stubble no particular place to go

in a suit with a mic
at our daughter's wedding

    your shoulder against a dolly under something heavy

on I-5, on 880
talking, missing the exit

    your hands over the sink

on the keyboard
with hammer or x-acto or pen

    the current I stand in, its surge and drag

face in the mirror next to mine
day after day forgetting to really look at you
as if you would be here forever

The field of me twines with the field of you

Not field as in meadow, though you are a meadow of infinite
complexity, but as in force, as in space-time, as in electro-magnetism.
All these years of bumping up against, mixing and jostling, the you
molecules doing the taxes the me molecules doing the dishes or
vice versa, you drive, I drive, my fish soup, your chile, your thick
biography, my lopsided stacks of poetry, nightstands, nightmares,
comfort in the small hours, interweaving fingers instead of legs, still
sweet, with a dark, bitter edge, no longer even wondering what you
will think, already thinking it.

Shadow World

All day, slumped in waiting rooms or on the phone, between one worry
    and the next,
each requiring that I start with the spelling of my name, my date of birth,
    the recitation of the facts
till they become a sort of litany, the Mass in Latin or the Mourner's
    Kaddish, all day
in the arid interstices, I've been reading C. K. Williams, the way his lines
    unfold like the breath,
carry me with them, pierce the barely breathable air to remind me that
    beyond this reality
with its gritty windows that don't open, the year-old copies of People
    Magazine, the procedures, the follow-up tests,
there remains another, shadow world where trouble is transformed in a
    surge of words
so that even tarring a roof or regretting a past love emerges somehow
    glistening, that there is no human suffering
too mundane or too terrible to ponder, wonder at, turn over in the
    questing, restless brain —
dark grease on the finger, precision steel of the gears—to marvel at their
    intricate, implacable whirl
even when it's you caught in them.

Thinking of Peter

A week past the twenty-ninth anniversary of your death
I read Seamus Heaney's poem about the kite,
and my first thought is to show it to you.

So I stumble again
into the hole death leaves,
unfillable.

This dim morning
of a day that promises
to be beautiful
without your presence
except for this faint ache
because you loved kites,
their unpredictable dialog
with the wind
transmitted to your hand.

That hand gone
and gone again
each time
I reach for it.

Why I have a soft spot for bad TV

My father was mostly a remote figure in a suit and fedora who left early and came home late, telling us to turn off the lights or sweep the garage. But a few nights a week he would shed his jacket and tie, sit back in the nubby, beige Barcalounger, his shirt lightly rumpled and his face relaxed, and we kids would be on the floor for *Perry Mason* or *Ozzie and Harriet*. He would laugh at the corny jokes and cry real, soundless tears when Lassie came home. Sometimes I sat on his lap. My brothers stopped squabbling. What we had of peace was these few hours of bad TV we sat before as if by the flames of a campfire, practicing.

Another Morning on Earth

On the altar in the living room, pictures of my parents,
my brother at forty, Larry's parents,
my mother and her sisters on Atlantic City Boardwalk in the thirties,
and Erwin, my mother's last love, for the besotted, lively gaze
she turns on him, though I try to keep him
behind the flowers. Perhaps they watch me,
even watch over me. When I fell
and it was just bad enough
to put up railings and walk more slowly,
I felt they had given me a warning.
Or when the baby is here, or when we gather,
or an ordinary morning,
newspaper or book or laptop, the ramekin of salt
on the table — there they are,
watching.

I change the flowers as they wilt,
alstroemerias, anemones, the last sweet peas,
because I want my dead to keep watching out for us,
for the children and grandchildren and beloved friends
in this chancy world where death lurks on the landing
or in the car, or microbes
or snipers or breast
or bone or stomach.

What do they think about the time I waste?
Such an abundance that I throw whole hours
into online Scrabble or Threes,
because it's hard to be here now,
now being a confused elixir
of sun and fog and email and bird shadow and superstition
and chicken feet and toast and news

and insatiable longing and I have to pee, a fusillade
of random moments that can converge
into a ravishing pattern,
which I have, from time to time and briefly, glimpsed.

But mostly I wander the planet with blinders on,
going somewhere fast.
I like to keep moving.
I like my time full.
And I like to believe that because

their photos look out from their niche
in the living room, they are present, and if
I keep a fresh parade of flowers on the altar
they will keep on keeping me
from harm.

Dark Shell

Looseplex 21: Nancy, an Elegy

Nancy, her cats. Fawns browse the backyard.
Fragments of the past in a kaleidoscope

      No moment entirely free of shadow.
      A woman who inhabits her space,

Veins, scars, hands molded from fixing things.
Five crows flap down the dawn street and land.

      Shards of a favorite rough brown cup,
      Persistent attentiveness to each moment,

A sense of grace above the kitchen table.
Day follows day without my intervention.

      Slipped so completely from this garment of skin.
      What makes sweet peas smell like longing?

Gorse buds snap in the hot afternoon.
Acres of gold-brown weeds disrobing.

After

At first, to be alive is all you need.
The sweet bitterness of coffee,
the hand with the umbrella,
the blanket's warmth
as you step from the wing of the plane
afloat on icy water
onto the deck of the rescue boat.
Even the air's acrid sting
on the skin of your cheeks
is welcome.

But soon
you begin to miss your laptop,
your keys, the numbers
stored in your phone.
This is the daily wonder,
to take life for granted
each time
it's restored to you.

Being here now

black-hearted bleak-outlooked I crisscross the urban stop-light-
ridden traffic-choked terrain and am late and drive badly not
polite not patient passing my disgruntlement to others driving
near me who spread it further a drop of toxic dye in the already
damaged pond we share and I see and acknowledge my small
part in making the day worse for everyone and yet any attempt to
deflect or reflect not going to make it no poetic intimations no veil
lifting from my eyes no clearer purer vision of reality just stuck
in this slightly sweaty body in the here and now out-of-sorts and
behind the wheel

Equivocal Activist

It's Friday. We pull out of the Paris climate accord
and I get my hair cut as Aretha bridges
troubled water. I could lay me down,
but I doubt that would accomplish anything.
Would anything accomplish anything?
Still, I'm uncomfortable doing nothing,
an equivocal activist, pretty sure
I can't count on my teammates,
jumpy as a handful of BBs
dropped on stone.

I can see how restful it would be
to believe in the simple solution.

Instead, heavy-footed,
I tread the Earth, while the sun rises
and sets without comment
and the chickens, remorseless,
search out any protein around,
even if it's the last Doloff cave spider
and dragonflies ricochet above us
stitching the tattered sky
while I do what passes for
the best I can.

Sleepwalking

Each night sleep asserts its mysterious imperative
as the mind ceases to brace itself
against its own undoing, against what lurks in the back
of the dark, the bad luck
and extraordinary privilege
of human being: water protein marrow fat, those
convolutes of DNA that say
bleary blue bright brown iris
say barrel legs willow stalks, hair that never grays,
canny fingers, tricky thinking.

And even though it doesn't feel like I am merely plasma
in a permeable membrane interacting with air and water
and prejudice and language into which mist
I find myself plunked,
occasionally I glimpse
that it's true, everything fluid,
everything affecting everything else
so that the racist rants of the attacker in Portland
infuse a gritty particulate into the common air,
cold bone fragments make it hard to breathe,
many small knives press against the very flesh of my very neck,
and everywhere clamor, the scrabble for or against
rage, righteousness, acts analyzed
and repudiated,
but here and now
before sleep comes to claim me
with its car wrecks and crumbling teeth, I acknowledge
that I understand nothing,
not on any team
and on every team at once, connected,
for better and worse
to everything.

How can you tell when someone's lying?

because unlike Pinocchio, the nose
stays the same size
doesn't even twitch
and the eyes find yours
with great earnestness
and the polygraph is
hardly better than a coin flip
and trained interrogators
can't do much better
despite all that body language interpretation
because the best liars
first convince themselves
and then convince you

but apparently
in the process
their vocabulary shrinks
and unique words
get scarce
as tits on a fish

they can only repeat
the same story
with the same words
while someone who tells what we call
the truth
wades through
bright cascades of memory,
shimmer and echo and nuance,

delicately calibrated emotion
the memory recreating
the experience
while the liar
stays locked
in the poverty
of the lie.

Penis Envy

Of course I want one.

The way it squats
at the center,
always ready to hand.

The way it rises
from the root,
unbidden.

No wonder men
have troubles,
that fat shaft

always
wanting more.

wishes for lawmakers

for lucille clifton

let them be pregnant
each man and woman of them.
let them be sick
and spooked

and clueless.
let every clinic
that could help
be closed.

let every doctor be barred
from discussing it.

let them try
bitter herbs and jumping.
let them consider
coat hangers
and grimy knives.

as their mouth fills
with the coppery spit of despair
let them stand before
lawmakers not unlike themselves
who rule against them.

What $7,000 could buy in 2007

The bones of Alastair Cooke, his body awaiting cremation
Information on who abused and abandoned a pit bull in Florida
A designer alligator-skin handbag
A high quality video-conferencing system
Rapper Keith Murray's stolen laptop with his life's work
A scholarship for a kilt-wearing, bagpipe-playing college freshman
Donated human eggs from a healthy non-smoker between 20 and 27
Plastic surgery to create six-pack abs
The assassination of Benazir Bhutto

Perfect Balance

We imagine
a world of perfect harmony

We imagine imagining
how the lion

lies down with the Xbox
as the dragon needle

of dread
ceases its endless stitching.

We imagine this, strapped
to the wheel of this world

as it creaks
against sinew and nerve

where the work is to grasp
perfection

in every terrible turn.

Corporate Ode

How we love to hate them,
their manifold billions buying up
the rainforest, belching smoke, polluting the river.
We hate their hierarchies, their patrimony,
their thumb heavy on the most vulnerable spot.
We hate them as we drive the car engineered
in Germany, manufactured in nine countries in seven time zones, in four
body styles, with seven engine options and three transmissions, sold
in more than 151 countries, against a backdrop of edgy,
autocratic governments, arcane regulations and vastly different
expectations of labor and management.

We hate them as we text our kids that we'll be late,
as we check directions, get guided to the door,
as we push the loaded cart down the aisle,
as we order in, order out, order online.
We hate them as we tie the laces of the perfectly molded
shoe, as we zip the cunning zipper on the sleeping bag,
snap the tent into place in 60 seconds, as we reach
with a click beyond the earth's atmosphere
to a whirling sphere
that instantly connects
to the distant one we long for,
to see the beloved face
to hear the unique voice
to almost touch them

The Tenth Time

Nirvana is here, nine times out of ten
Hô Xuân Hu'o'ng

The disposable diaper
in the meadow

The morning at the DMV

The razor wire on top of the chainlink
around the concrete
around the school

For every black man in college
five behind bars

What happens to the eyes
as the argument flares

The blueprints for the gas chambers,
meticulously filed

The invasion

The story of the invasion

The story behind the story
of the invasion

The ones
who knew to profit from it

Passenger Tenderness

At the reading, the poet's words come faster than you can grasp
competing as they do with your internal cacophony
as you remember the laptop and cell phone
behind the unlocked car's seat,
too late now to get up.
In the poem,
balconies gleam white.
White light and shadow
define the needles of the pine.

It's hard to feel affection
for the woman in line who made you late
wanting recompense for her rotten avocado,
though certainly the poet's compassion for the others
on his airplane, passenger tenderness,
applies to us all
as we stumble along this confusing passage,
murky at both ends, mostly murky in the middle,
a few moments brilliantly outlined:
the white balcony,
the pine needle's shadow,
the jagged silhouette of barnacles on
memory's exposed pier.

But most of it's rudderless,
the passage ongoing since long before you joined it
crammed with objects hauled in trunks across oceans,
dragged on wagons, stored and tended and passed down
with remedies and stories and recipes
and ways of looking at the world
that permeate your vision
so that it takes a lifetime
to try to unravel what you see,

and you discover yourself wandering
the fluorescent aisles
choosing white candles because red is too goyish,
startled by the layers of cultural insanity
that produced that judgment.

Meanwhile, the sadness of the poem

> *You can fall a long way in sunlight.*
> *You can fall a long way in the rain.*

expands inside you
the way the skin of water
spilled on a table stretches
to absorb the drop next to it
and the next, because each year
more are gone, till
the edges of the pool
are no longer visible.

You can remember what it was like
to wake on a summer morning
before anything really bad had happened
to you personally, and the blackberries
fattened in the sun against the hot tar roof
of the rented cottage.

And now the poet conjures the scent of lilacs,
the small, star-shaped blossoms falling
onto the waves of a shore
you've never seen, and you quiet
your interior monolog for a moment
and breathe their smell:
lilac, lilac, lilac.

Sándor Márai in San Diego

Deprived of the Magyar language, of pörkölt simmered
in cramped kitchens, of the scent of elderflowers,
you don't meet cronies on the street. You scour
the shops; they don't sell what you need. You wander
through cafés — there's no one here you know,
no one to gossip with, to disentangle
your braided consonants. The war mangled
your world—the Germans set up radios
in your parlor, Reds used it for their motor pool.
Your bones crave cold light, Krisztinaváros,
the stones of Castle Hill, the view from Sparrow
Tower before the siege. You need the cruel
tartness of accented vowels. This southern sun
can't melt the bullets of your native tongue.

Looseplex: Tsunami

It was morning for days afterward.
The telephone poles and wires whipped and sparked.

    Gold looked like brass and bones poked up through plowed fields.
    You can fall a long way in sunlight.

The white balcony, the pine needle's shadow
Impossibly doomed and graceful and obsessed.

    Is the psyche bound to the body?
    Icing of debris over orderly fields,

Barnacles on memory's exposed pier.
The way pain fades to the memory of pain

    Slicing the orange flesh of the papaya.
    O life, life, you are such a muchness!

I searched for more footage of the massive waves.
It was mourning for days afterward.

Brief Poems on Physics

Looseplex : Losing Patience

How many years was my path obscured by junk
My ungovernable heart, pocked with grievance?

> Microorganisms effervesce
> Starting from something simple, like milk.

Push up bras, slim jims, and cheese doodles
Endlessly stitching snags in the sky.

> Remember being crazed with desire?
> Seeds release in heat, the ground charred clear for them.

We talk after dinner, wine glasses refilled.
The monks who touched the match to their own dowsed robes.

> What I believed was the absolute truth, no.
> The fluorescent, merciless present.

The earth gearing up to shrug us off,
These are the stamps on the final envelope.

Made of molecules

I take for granted that the earth is solid the idea of permanence
seductive as I move about checking the time going here going there
the small chores and pleasures of daily interaction shaken when
the lanterns in the Hunan restaurant suddenly begin to sway and
we run outside remembering that the reliable ground under our
feet can suddenly shift that the live oak with its wrinkled elephant
trunk and ancient lichen its catkins and acorns reassembles itself
moment to moment as if forever as if predictable as if not vulner-
able as if not a continuous regrouping a notion a casual kiss that
might be the last

why humans?

for the joke, even the pun,
for black humor in a bleak hour,
for the complication of stuff: tangled,
woven, manufactured, compressed, crooked,
cooked, plastic and rubber and Corian,
concrete, steel and asphalt,
for glass blown
from sand and fire,
for grammar, for the 6,500 spoken languages,
for mensch and derrière and giggle and preposterous,
for the winch, the pulley, the level, the wheel,
for faucets that turn on when you wave your hand,
for hands, for their cunning thumbs,
for false teeth,
false testimony, avarice,
compassion, for the known step
of the beloved on the stairs,
arched eyebrow, gap tooth, elfin ear,
for arrival, for departure,
the longing for return,
for the embrace,
the howl, the song,
for the brief spark
in the spiraling
dark

Thinking about Einstein while waiting for the Big Blue Bus

how it is that the light at the corner of Pico and Lincoln that spills so
generously over sidewalk blue metal chairs five lanes with their cross-
stitch of traffic can be "discrete packets, discontinuous, distributed
across space" how could a mind on a series of ordinary mornings
forkfuls and mouthfuls and earfuls deconstruct the everywhereness
of light into microscopic moving parts some of which only exist
when they bump into each other how could he gaze at the golden
abundance spilling over Ulm and Munich and Pavia and think no
not a blanket not a swath but a gathering of particles that meander
somewhat predictably through the bent universe to bump against
us in leaps and bounces while in Germany the Jews begin to stitch
yellow stars on their sleeves and next to me at the bus stop mostly
Hispanic faces and the light streaming over everyone

Eleven Daffodils

What am I to make
of these daffodils,
perfumed strumpets, picked
who knows where
by who knows whom
possibly genetically
modified, commercially
fertilized, spritzed
with pesticide?

These questions did not arise
when I tossed
the budded stems
in my shopping cart
on a chill afternoon:
essence of spring
for a dollar twenty-nine.

Now they sit
and radiate scent,
molecules of daffodil
mix with molecules of oxygen
around my desk
until I am dizzy
with praise
and regret.

More about the oak

It dominates the view its branches so inviting that the first thing we
did was make a treehouse inside them not worried about the oak
not thinking about the way each leathery leaf turns air and sunlight
and water into food and draws the water another nanometer up
through the channel of xylem from roots that reach deep so the
trunk becomes a great reservoir and during the eight dry months of
a California spring and summer and fall lets gravity pull some of its
aquifer back to nourish the shallow roots around it not considering
the network of rhizomes this small ecosystem of hillside not really
seeing the oak at all except as ornament as tool for our human
pleasure and it tolerates us as the treehouse falls into disuse and
the squirrels and crows and sentinel hummingbirds survey their
territory from its branches as the small humans who played there
move on

Grammar

When Nietzsche said we no longer need God
because we have grammar, he was talking about

a morning like this one. The rain has finally paused
and patches of intermittent radiance play over the washed world

illuminating first the water, then the bridge,
then the towers of the city that gleam white

before a focused mist, like a celestial
garden hose, sprays a single patch of downtown

with a filmy, golden gauze. To top it off, the light
glides over the Golden Gate and creates a rainbow

smack between the orange towers, opening
upward to a vault of lapidary blue.

And the brain hums and leaps, inserting pattern
and meaning into this display, because grammar itself,

every word we use demands it, the way we need a story
to justify why we did whatever we did,

the way we insert divine intent
into every random raindrop.

Dirac's equation

now when I watch the milk heat up on the gas burner I know that heat agitates the electrons, making each spin a little faster around the heavy nucleus of milk fat, so the surface of the milk begins to ruffle and swell and little explosions escape at the edges and I am wondering as I pour the hot milk into my coffee about the long streams of red and yellow lights I sometimes watch, looking down from the hill above the freeway at the evening commute those blinking rivers of individual cars that stretch far into the darkening evening, what agitation moves among us pushes us here and there in some possibly mathematically predictable spectrum while we think we are going somewhere

Jung on Dying

Is the psyche bound to the body?
Jung thinks not.
In dreams
the psyche travels
unconstrained by matter.
As for death, the unconscious
rejects it.

Those who live as if
the rich cloth of time
were unrolling endlessly before them
are better off.
It's not a question of belief.

We need salt, he says,
does it matter why?
Food tastes better with it.

Matvei Petrovich Bronstein

there is the ability to look into what we call empty space and
visualize and calibrate its true nature and there is the pot of
beans neglected while you scribble at the kitchen table as it boils
up and over to congeal around the burner in a crusty sludge
the shift between deciphering the loops of quantum gravity and
the grave political landscape in which you also exist the one in
which the surviving prisoner recalls that Matvei distracted them
with lectures on science while they waited for the next round of
interrogation and blows and that he knew the most poems by heart
of any prisoner

The Conservation of Matter

I follow the hump of the whale exhaling
as it heads for the Bering Sea. I want to see it, and see it again,

closer. Or branches in a storm, their exuberant dance
with the wind. Even rain on a New York street,

cigarette butts in the gutter, taxis splattering. I can't get enough of it.
You say: When we die we cease to exist. Everything else

is illusion. But what about that law of physics:
the conservation of matter? How water changes to

steam or ice—mass plus energy
equal to the first wet splash.

And our hard-won companionship, smelted
in a blaze of day after day?

The dead look out from their accustomed photos,
stopped in time, but not altogether silent,

as the last whiff of the whale's breath
transforms into ocean, air.

Lying on the massage table at the mudbaths

after twelve minutes immersed in a tub of hot volcanic mud and
twelve minutes in a bath of hot mineral water my heart thumps against
the padded surface and I remember that I exist thanks to this mostly
unremarked heart a thermodynamic system that chugs along blood
in blood out every artery vein tiny capillary breathe in leafy oxygen
breathe out CO_2 and I understand with my hot pumping body that
what I call self is inextricable from the body here on this table the
flannel blanket absorbing particles of me as I slowly cool the New Age
music bothering my sensibility like a persistent gnat the laugh track
last night on the rerun of Friends the forgotten French vocabulary and
Pythagorean Theorem the anxieties waiting to swarm when I return
to my usual state every encounter and memory since my small hot self
emerged on this planet till the engine finally stops and I cool for good
and the cells of me transform into earth ash air as my spirit into yours
as you read these words

Spring and All

Looseplex: Despite everything, spring

No one was watching. We searched the silence
Like a farmer in drought, ears open for rain.

    Each morning, each evening, scatter of yellow.
    Whatever else may occur, it's spring,

A framework for the rags of this world,
Real joy mixed with a certain uncertainty.

    Overnight a fuzz of tender green.
    It glints and shimmers. It pulls me towards it — strong

Carpet of newborn shoots under last year's weeds.
Five billion miles away, a galaxy dies.

    Aretha's hat, Yo Yo Ma's delight,
    Is this our work, to love what is here?

To move along the skin of this earth
Married like enamel to the tooth.

March in California

All week blossoms, black branch brilliant in white flower foam,
whole trees startle in shades of pink.

This is what ball gowns aim for:
shape made glorious by perfect ornament.

Underfoot, everywhere, petals: pink confetti
mixes with trash on a San Francisco sidewalk,

white flakes blow back from car wheels,
petals drift over fields of mustard flowers.

At the market, among eleven eggs in shades of brown,
the first duck egg, pale and perfectly oval, larger than the rest,

an egg that makes you think: duckling. The orange yolk
a medium for organs and feathers, webs of feet, a beak

to crack the shell open from inside. Life
frying in my pan, while outside, trees in their designer gowns

perfect and disposable,
the party, once again, just begun.

Bulb

what's left
after flower, leaves, stalk

lump of pure desire

in darkness
deprived of dirt

roots stretch

I want
to be like that

Two Haiku

Metaphor

> The earth as a
> drop dead gorgeous woman
> with bad taste in men.

Bikini Ode

> How artfully it
> draws the eye to just those parts
> it's meant to hide

What is the matter with plain old cause-and-effect?

The burden of uncertainty,
how it can ruin even a tulip,
how the weight of it
makes taking care of an infant
unendurable,
the tedium and vague distress,
hour after hour of it:
milk, sleep, worry, repeat.

Luckily, there are always puppies.

At the edge of your vision,
clouds mass like news,
the endless terrible,
somewhere someone burning,
real but not really real.

The stranger introduces himself,
does that make him any less strange?
Even marrying him?

And time, too,
that *winged whatchamacallit.*

The jerky pattern
raindrops make down the windshield
persists, past, present, pluperfect,
future perfect.

After the storm, golden
fish and chips. The juncos flash
their wet white tails.
Worms rise
through damp soil. Delight
flits along the veins.

The Worm Within

Earthworms have
no ears or eyes,
yet shy
from the footfall of birds
and are especially
sensitive to
the presence
of their enemy, the mole.
When Darwin serenaded worms
with a bassoon,
they would respond
with a satisfying wriggle,
the way we,
too, may vibrate
to mysterious promptings,
too obscure
to label.

Dawn

an apricot moon broods over the bay
then disappears

on the hill
two fawns and a doe
browse the damp grass,
ears twitching

the newspaper waits
at the curb
the morning
fears still unwrapped

tea steeps red brown in the pot

Art

the body in surrounding air defined by its relationship to that
air as the image of Amelia at eleven in her straight-backed ballet
pose poised to levitate slightly above the wooden floor as though
gravity no longer fully applies can't compete with her youth
and discipline and delight or Egon Schiele's *Reclining Nude with
Raised Torso* the same quality of body in space drawn with such
tenderness that the curls of her hair the roundness of breast and
shoulder reproduced on the wall calendar comfort me a hundred
years after he sketched them how art enriches this battered earth
our poisonous particulates transcends in purity of line and intent
if only for the moment our endless permutations of evil the body
humming with what we might call divine what a run we've had
what a run

Consider the Fig

Why do poets praise the black art
of the berry when the fig stars
flat leaves like a talisman,
slips onto the outstretched palm?
A one-thumbed glove,
the fig has nothing to prove.
Soft as a scrotum,
silken from top to bottom,
smug as a full house
where wasps drowse
and raccoons wait
to plunder by night.

Spun gloss, concentrate
of lush long days: late
slanted shadows, sleepy forms
sprawled in parents' arms,
toys scattered, lawn chairs akimbo,
hammocks swinging empty. Slow
dusk drapes the landscape
as it cools. Fig seeds detonate
on the tongue in one last bright
blaze of honeyed light.

Two Cinquains

Bee in the Epiphyllum

From squat
slabs of cactus
they flame up, these giant
scentless siren calls. Even I
want in.

The Deliciousness of Return

Garden
gone wild, breakfast
of zucchini flowers.
The world opens again, with me
in it.

Dollars and Sense

Forty years ago
when we were down to our last fifty cents,
our friends drove up
with a month's rent and groceries,
and after we ate and talked, we sat together
on the edge of the dock, saying nothing,
as we watched the barnacles
slowly open their feathery lips,
slowly close them.

Forever

You might be standing in a tide pool
as an anemone feathers
each wave.

Or you might be lost
in corn stubble as far as the horizon
while a chorus of crickets
scrape their fiddle legs
into the expanding silence.

Or you might be impatient
on a corner in New York
waiting for the traffic to pass,
when suddenly
the intricate grain of the sidewalk
comes alive under your shoes,
the air hums with multiple destinations,
the shop windows' seductive invitations,
the crisscross of lives briefly intersecting,
and you stand there
while the light changes
again and again.

Praise

Looseplex: Praise

Apparently nothing happened in April,
More like lichen, the way it fastens on stone.

> How time stretches, how light bends—how
> Trout go for the glitter of the hand-tied fly,

A shaft of light falling on the page.
Quiet joy seeps in with wakefulness,

> The ficus greens by the air conditioner.
> The incessant OM of cars on 880.

Gravity, force that through the green fuse.
Anther and filament, tiny winged seeds?

> Throw in the towel, pick up the trowel,
> Death, too, can dazzle: a brilliant flame and then

Finish the job and turn into gossamer.
Exit this life into ashes and pure air.

Silver Lining

How lucky I am
to suffer, not
as infants and
invertebrates do,
in the moment
only, but
suffering
that endures
in anticipation,
in retrospect,
pain that lives with me
like a bad tooth,
the way it makes me
chew on the other
side of my mouth,
the way the tongue
can't leave it alone,
each careful bite
so risky,
so delicious.

Why There Is No Name for the Divine

The Hebrews were right, insisting
God is nameless
incomprehensible as the baby
at the end of the bayonet
or the eyes of the eighteen-year-old
at the other end
or his mother's eyes
scanning the long road, waiting
for word
of him.

The divine holds them all
and sings,
like this minute rag of yellow
among the weed seeds
above the freeway
that we, compelled
to name almost everything, call
goldfinch.

Leda's Dream

All self-consciousness drops from her
the way the seams of a dress unravel at the shoulders.
How could she have known
the swan would be a perfect lover?
The long neck
snakes to its black beak.
The many small sharp teeth,
the heavy webs of the toes
do not scare her,
though violence is part of it.
And the feathers,
the possibilities of feathers
she couldn't have guessed.

What Birds Know

Researchers who must kill their animals to study them
call this sacrifice, just as the Greeks
sacrificed a bull to Apollo for safe journey,
so the metaphor survives
though the mouse dies.

Always our animal companions
exist at our pleasure—
the fattened hog
roasting on the spit,
the shorn sheep in the field.

Chickens thrive on grain
we spread for them.
The birds of the air
observe
and steer clear

In Praise of Research

Here's to the researchers' necks arched over their microscopes
with the single-mindedness of a horse bent to its oats
hour after year in the chemical room of the lab
decoding the origin of a sub-family of mosquito
that only lives sealed in the London underground,
or Marie Curie burning her hands over and over
in the beautiful blue-green glow of the radium she extracted
before anyone knew it was there
or what it could do,
or the scholar holed up in the library carrel
working on the meaning of a semicolon.
Quinine, x-rays, meaning itself, the way
that time stretches and light bends
and like horses in traces
impelled by the will of our kind
we bend our necks to it
as hungry for knowledge
as for grain from a loving hand.

Haibun for Amanda

Waking at 4:22am, curled between Larry and the cats, I luxuriate in the thought of you across the bay, unspooling from the seduction of the bed's warmth to gather your gear and head for the surf. I imagine the pull of the bed at war with the pull of the waves till you give in to the waves and rise. What do you put on? An old swimsuit? Sweats? A scarf? Do you throw a big towel over your shoulder and leave the big-toothed zipper of the neoprene till you hit the beach? Do you wear booties, gloves, a cap? I ponder these questions as I slide out between warm bodies to pee and am rewarded by the almost orange orb of the full moon sliding into view between the branches of the oak. How bright it must be over the ocean, a lush, glittering, golden path that disappears as you enter it.

Isn't this, too, love?
why have we been so stingy
with definitions?

In praise of cheating

who
hasn't
cheated
a bit? slid
the office pen
into the personal
pocket relished a piece
of toast not on the diet or
as you track the experiment
shade the numbers just a fraction
and to cheat on your partner makes
sex much hotter everyone cheats on their
taxes cheat on the test cheat at cards cheat
your friend cheat on the lover that you're cheating
on your partner with the batter uses steroids the boxer
takes a dive the broker makes insider trades as a child you
first learn the thrill of it the ability to fool is so grownup
that you can put one over the deliciousness of risk
balanced by the shame of getting caught   heat
rising to your face what contempt we have
for Nixon a man who cheated even at golf
you have to cheat to know that utterly
slimy feeling you double-dealing
underhanded wretch you've
brought dishonor to your
race how could you
really how
could you
not?

No Whining

I prefer the example of Sam Lopata,
whose father died in Auschwitz. He grew up
broke in Paris then designed restaurants in NY.
His favorite was the "love in the ruins" look:
a perfectly finished dining room
bludgeoned by a wrecking crew,
dangling wires and rubble around the tables.
Life goes on — he said — *you go into the wreck
and have fun. Get it?*

Ode to Flatulence

Even the word fart is funny, plosive, puffed from the tongue.

Children adore them in any form, especially when gas bubbles up in the
    tub, ebullient, visible.

And fart jokes and frat boys a perfect concordance.

For new lovers, to fart in bed the shyest first risk of exposure.

The perfectly private pleasure, almost sexual, when a large, ripe one rumbles
    down the anal canal, released from the radiating folds of the small,
    slit-like aperture, to sing its relief.

Or the opposite thrill, legs splayed in the packed yoga class or butt bared
    on massage table, the delight of restraint, spiced with a sort of dread,
    soldiers tense at the gates.

At work in your cube, you hope your coworkers might somehow believe it
    was somebody else, as the stink lingers in a foul cloud like a thought
    balloon, its little bubble stem pointed directly at you.

Yes, the fart is the ultimate joke, fetid as whale breath, no pretense
    possible as it spouts from the hole we don't mention.

How the ability not to
lets everyone know you are versed in the ways of your tribe,
no longer a baby, out of control and beloved,
or even a toddler, taking the first steps toward shame.
When you can hold your fart, you are a person, too,
however small, however new to the trade,
someone who does what people do,
someone who knows how to wait.
Someone whose butt's on straight.

Endless Chores Ode

Drifts of laundry spilled along the couch, sink
stifled with dishes, no counter
that doesn't need wiping, stove top
layered in magma, don't even open the oven door.
The surprise of cat shit in the closet, dust bunnies
instead of lust. And even if
I clean it all up, if I summon
the energy and focus to get it
for one moment under control, as soon
as I put the last glass on the shelf and go
for a walk, it starts all over again,
the sink full by the time I get back.
And the repetitive, ineffectual
nagging that goes with it,
so that I am the harridan,
the hag of chores. The tyranny
of this life of scrubber and rag,
need and need and need the basso ostinato,
the ambient drone of the ever undone
a mountain of sound I am stuck under,
struggling for oxygen, desperate
for one uncluttered spot, my only escape
a wormhole to paid work.
How many years was my path
obscured by junk? When did I first
stand at the sink at peace
with the suds and the crud?
When did the house stop seething, the floors
steady a bit? Was it the day
we made shortbread and cleaned up

together, eating the buttery squares
from the pan? Maybe the day
I discovered the beat in the broom,
the dance of the daily, Aretha pulsing
through all the unplanned griefs and loss,
the failures, the terrible,
unpredictable phone calls, the relief
of something to do, my familiar,
my reliable, stalwart companion,
always available, when nothing else
is getting me through.

The Muse Talks Back

Poetry didn't grab me by the hair and sit me down and say "You must write." It was more a flirtation, or no, more of a family member, familiar, always present, beloved, exasperating, neglected. Often neglected. Diapers, meals, rent, measuring cardamom, cinnamon, mace, a lesson in how to solder a join in copper pipe. The work of words always last on the list.

Now that time has opened and I turn to that slighted sylph, that elusive goddess, she laughs, her golden ringlets obscuring her features.

"Suffer for me," she demands.
"Relearn everything.
I demand nothing less."

Part of the Spirit

There is a part of the spirit that cannot be destroyed.

Dean Young

But which part? The part that makes you pull over
to help the couple stranded by the side of the freeway,
or the part that's relieved they don't need you?
The part that obsesses over poisons and warming
or the part that rejoices as dawn slowly illumines the canyon?

And what, even, is spirit?
Something not subject to decay,
that shifts, changes,
can't be held? the way a wave
can lift, drift, expand and brighten,
grind to sand?
iridescent, evanescent?

The snatch of song that lingers
in the man you taught as a boy
so he thinks of you
as he sits at the keys
and his fingers remember?

A touch that gives comfort
even after the hand is gone?

Borrowed Time

The moon is a flashlight
on my face.
It wakes me with its
interrogating light.
To its accusations
I have no answer.
Perhaps I will go on
living on this earth.

About the Author

Meryl Natchez' most recent book is a bilingual volume of translations from the Russian: *Poems From the Stray Dog Café: Akhmatova, Mandelstam and Gumilev.* She is co-translator of *Tadeusz Borowski: Selected Poems.* Her book of poems, *Jade Suit,* appeared in 2001. Her work has appeared in *The Hudson Review, Poetry Northwest, The American Journal of Poetry,* ZYZZYVA, *The Pinch Literary Review, Atlanta Review, Lyric, The Moth, Comstock Review,* and many others. She is on the board of Marin Poetry Center. Ms. Natchez has had a career as a technical writer. She founded and managed a technical writing business, TechProse, now owned and managed by the employees. She co-founded the non-profit, Opportunity Junction, now in its 15th year, and raised four children. She blogs at www.dactyls-and-drakes.com.

A Note on the Type

The typeface used for the text of the poems is Janson, an old-style serif face designed by Miklós Tótfalusi Kis (1650–1702). Its name comes from Anton Janson (1620–1687), a printer from the Netherlands, who was originally thought to be the creator of the type. The face used for poem titles is Brandon Grotesque, a typeface designed by Hannes von Döhren of Berlin in 2009 for the HvD Type Foundry.

Longship Press

Longship Press is an independent small-press publishing house located in San Rafael, California. It is the publisher of the literary journal *Nostos.* The principal editor is Lawrence Tjernell who may be reached via lawrence.tjernell@longshippress.com.